WATER BATH CANNING AND PRESERVING COOKBOOK FOR BEGINNERS

ENJOY FINEST RECIPES WITH YOUR FAVORITE DISHES

By

Sweet Daisy

Table of Content

Jam and Jellies 1

    1.   Peach Spice Jam 1

    2.   Blackberry Jam 3

    3.   Mandarin Orange Jam 4

    4.   Cherry Jam 6

    5.   Apple Pie Jam 8

    6.   Nectarine Brown Sugar Jam 10

    7.   Strawberry Jam 11

    8.   Lime Mint Jelly 13

Pickles 15

    9.   Pickled Garlic scrapes 15

    10.   Pickled Pullet Eggs 17

    11.   Canned Spicy Garlic Pickled Carrots 19

    12.   Sweet and Spicy Pickled Radishes 21

    13.   Pickled Bean Salad 23

    14.   Sweet Pickles 25

    15.   Pickled Green Beans 27

    16.   Christmas Pickled Morsels 29

    17.   Pickled Sweet-Sour Squash 31

18.   Giardiniera 32

19.   Apple-Walnut Maple Conserve 34

20.   Strawberry Pectin Jam 36

21.   Honey-Lavender Peaches 38

22.   Apple Pie Filling 40

23.   Pineapple Peach Spread 42

24.   Fresh Berries 43

25.   Berry Syrup 45

Vegetables **47**

26.   Tomato with Hot Pepper 47

27.   Crushed Tomato 49

28.   Quick Pickled Red Onions 50

29.   Kale 52

30.   Turnips 54

31.   Mushroom 55

32.   Easy Cabbage Salads 56

33.   Stewed Tomatoes and Vegetables 57

34.   Almond Apricot Jam 59

Salsa and Sauces **61**

35.   Tangy Cranberry Sauce 61

36.   Spaghetti Sauce with Tomato 63

37.   Autumn Pepper Salsa 66

38.   Pear Sauce 68

39.   Apple Sauce 70

40.   Mango Salsa 73

41.   Fresh Green Salsa 74

42.	Corn, Avocado and Tomato Salsa 76

Marmalades **78**

43.	Lemon Honey Marmalade 78

44.	Strawberry Marmalade 79

45.	Onion Marmalade 81

46.	Pear Marmalade 82

47.	Tangy Navel Orange Marmalade 84

48.	Blueberry Orange Marmalade 86

49.	Kumquats Marmalade 88

50.	Orange Marmalade 90

51.	Onion Garlic Marmalade 91

52.	Three-Fruit Marmalade 93

53.	Orange Pineapple Marmalade 95

54.	Cherry Marmalade 97

Chutneys **99**

55.	Rhubarb Chutney 99

56.	Mango Chutney 100

57.	Rhubarb Cherry Chutney 102

58.	Raisin Pear Chutney 104

59.	Cucumber Relish with Pepper 105

60.	Mango Chutney with Raisin 107

61.	Garlicky Lime Chutney 109

62.	Pungent Tomato Pear Chutney 111

63.	Cilantro Chutney Recipe 113

64.	Indian Apple Chutney 114

65.	Plum Tomato Chutney 117

66. Curried Apple Chutney 118

67. Fruit Chutney 120

68. Green Tomato Chutney 122

69. Cantaloupe Chutney 123

70. Spicy Green Tomato Chutney 126

71. Black Currant 129

72. Watermelon Lemon 131

73. Tangy Tomato 132

74. Delicious Strawberry Preserve 135

Jam and Jellies

1. Peach Spice Jam

Preparation: time: 5 minutes

Cooking time: 15-25 minutes

Servings: 2-pint jars

Ingredients:

- 8-9 large peaches, pitted

- 3 cups sugar

- Juice and rind of 1/2 lemon

- 1/4 teaspoon allspice (optional)

- 1/4 teaspoon cloves (optional)

Directions

1) Detach pits and imperfect parts from peaches.

2) In a large kettle, parboil peaches with just enough water to keep them from burning. When peaches are softened, put them through a food mill.

3) To a deep saucepan or cooking pot, attach the peaches and enough water to submerge. Boil until softened. Drain water.

4) Transfer to a blender or food processor. Blend well to make puree.

5) To the pot or pan, add the puree and other ingredients.

6) Boil the mixture till thermometer reads 220F; cook over medium low heat until firm and thick. Swirl continually to prevent scorching.

7) Spill the hot mixture into pre-sterilized jars directly or with a jar funnel. Keep headspace of 1/4 inch from the jar top.

8) To detach tiny air bubbles, set a nonmetallic spatula and swirl the mixture gently.

9) Wipe the sealing edges. Secure the jars with the lids and adjust the bands/rings to seal and prevent any leakage.

10) Set the jars in a cool, dry and dark place. Allow them to cool down completely.

11) Store in your refrigerator for later use.

Nutrition:

- Calories: 435

- Protein: 5.1g

- Carbs: 11.4g

- Fat: 1.4g

- Sugar: 86.3g

2. Blackberry Jam

Preparation: time: 15 minutes

Cooking time: 30 minutes

Servings: 10-pint jars

Ingredients:

- 5 cups blackberries

- 2 cups sugar

- 2 tablespoons lemon juice

Directions:

1) Sterilize the bottles in a water bath canner. Allow the bottles to cool.

2) Place all ingredients in a saucepan. Set to a boil while stirring constantly for 10 minutes. Reduce the heat to simmer until the sauce thickens.

3) Set off the heat and allow to cool slightly.

4) Transfer the mixture to sterilized bottles and remove the air bubbles. Close the lid.

5) Set in a water bath canner and process for 10 minutes.

6) Consume within a year.

Nutrition:

- Calories: 196

- Protein: 1.7g

- Carbs: 49.7g

- Fat: 0.2g

- Sugar: 44.9g

3. Mandarin Orange Jam

Preparation: time: 15 minutes

Cooking time: 22 minutes

Servings: 5 pint jars

Ingredients:

- 5 bottling jars with lid

- 2 pounds mandarin oranges, peeled and seeded (about 10 to 12 oranges)

- Juice from 1 lemon, freshly squeezed

- 1 cup sugar

Directions:

1) Sterilize the bottles in a water bath canner.

2) Chop the mandarin oranges roughly. Place the ingredients except the pectin in a pot and heat over medium flame. Stir constantly for 10 minutes to avoid burning at the bottom.

3) Stir in pectin and stir for another 2 minutes.

4) Set off the heat and allow to cool.

5) Transfer the orange jam into the sterilized bottles and make sure that there is 1/4 headspace left. Remove the air bubbles. Close the lid.

6) Place the bottles in the water bath canner. Process for 10 minutes.

7) Consume within a year.

Nutrition:

- Calories: 169

- Protein: 1.3g

- Carbs: 41.6g

- Fat: 0.2g

- Sugar: 35g

4. Cherry Jam

Preparation: time: 15 minutes

Cooking time: 60 minutes

Servings: 4 pint jars

Ingredients:

- 4 canning bottles

- 2 pounds cherries, stems removed and pitted

- 2 1/2 cups sugar

- Juice from 1 lemon, freshly squeezed

- 2 drops of almond extract

Directions:

1) Sterilize the bottles in a water bath canner. Allow the bottles to cool.

2) Place all ingredients in a saucepan and cook for 40 minutes or until the mixture thickens. Continue swirling to prevent the bottom from burning.

3) Turn off the heat and remove from the pot to slightly cool.

4) Transfer to the bottles. Remove the air bubbles and close the lid.

5) Set in a water bath canner and process for 10 minutes.

6) Consume within a year.

Nutrition:

- Calories: 331

- Protein: 1.9g

- Carbs: 83.6g

- Fat: 0.6g

- Sugar: 78.7 g

5. Apple Pie Jam

Preparation: time: 15 minutes

Cooking time: 27 minutes

Servings: 8 half pint jars

Ingredients:

- 6 canning bottles

- 4 cups diced apples

- 2 tablespoons lemon juice, freshly squeezed

- 1 1/4 teaspoon ground cinnamon

- 1/4 teaspoon ground ginger

- 1/4 teaspoon ground nutmeg

- 4 cups granulated sugar

- 1 cup packed brown sugar

- 1/2 teaspoon unsalted butter

- 1 box pectin

Directions:

1) Sterilize the bottles in a water bath canner. Allow the bottles to cool.

2) Place the apples, lemon juice, cinnamon, ginger, nutmeg, sugar, and butter in a saucepan.

3) Turn on the heat and allow simmering for 15 minutes. Stir in the pectin and simmer for 2 minutes. Keep swirling to avoid the

4) mixture from burning.

5) Turn off the heat to cool.

6) Transfer the mixture to sterilized bottles and remove the air bubbles. Close the lid.

7) Set in a water bath canner and process for 10 minutes.

8) Consume within a year.

Nutrition:

- Calories: 275

- Protein: 0.2g

- Carbs: 70.6g

- Fat: 0.3g

- Sugar: 66.9g

6. Nectarine Brown Sugar Jam

Preparation: time: 15 minutes

Cooking time: 25 minutes

Servings: 8 half pint jars

Ingredients:

- 6 to 8 canning bottles

- 4 pounds nectarines, peeled, seeded and chopped

- 1 1/2 cup brown sugar, lightly packed

- 4 tablespoons lemon juice

- 1/2 teaspoon cinnamon

- 1/4 teaspoon ground ginger

Directions:

1) Sterilize the bottles in a water bath canner. Allow the bottles to cool.

2) Place all ingredients in a big saucepan and bring to a rolling boil for 5 minutes. Set the heat to low and parboil for another 10 minutes. Keep stirring until the mixture thickens.

3) Set off the heat and allow to cool slightly.

4) Transfer the mixture to sterilized bottles and remove the air bubbles. Close the lid.

5) Bring in a water bath canner and process for 10 minutes.

6) Consume within a year.

Nutrition:

- Calories: 259

- Protein: 2.5g

- Carbs: 65.2g

- Fat: 0.8g

- Sugar: 58.1g

7. Strawberry Jam

Preparation: time: 15 minutes

Cooking time: 1 hour and 20 minutes

Servings: 4 half pint jars

Ingredients:

- 2 pints jar

- 2 pounds ripe strawberries, hulled and cleaned

- 2 1/2 cups sugar

- 1 tablespoon freshly squeezed orange juice

Directions:

1) Sterilize the bottles in a water bath canner. Allow the bottles to cool.

2) Chop the strawberries and place all ingredients in a large pan. Let it sit for an hour until the sugar is dissolves and the mixture become watery.

3) Heat over the stove using medium flame and bring to a boil. Make sure to stir constantly and mashing with the ladle to macerate. Cook for 10 minutes then allow to cool.

4) Place the strawberry jam in sterilized bottles.

5) Set in a water bath canner and process for 10 minutes.

6) Consumer within a year.

Nutrition:

- Calories: 318

- Protein: 1.6g

- Carbs: 80.2g

- Fat: 0.7g

- Sugar: 73g

8. Lime Mint Jelly

Preparation time: 10 minutes

Cooking time: 10 minutes

Servings: 5 pint jars

Ingredients:

- 4 cups sugar

- 1-3/4 cups water

- 3/4 cup lime juice

- 3 drops green food coloring

- 1 (3 oz.) package liquid fruit pectin

- 3 tbsp. chopped fresh mint leaves

- 1/4 cup grated lime zest

Directions:

1) In a large saucepan, combine lime juice, sugar, water, and food coloring. Bring to a rolling boil, stirring constantly.

2) Stir in lime zest pectin, and mint. Continue boiling for 1 minute, stirring constantly.

3) Remove from heat and get rid of foam.

4) Scoop the hot mixture into half-pint jars (hot sterilized), leaving 1/4-inch space of the top. Get rid of excess air bubbles; add hot mixture to adjust headspace. Wipe the rims. Close the lids and tighten.

5) Set boiling water in a canner and set in the jars until fully covered. Allow to boil for 10 minutes. Set the jars aside to cool.

Nutrition:

- Calories 79

- Fat: 0 g

- Carbs: 21 g

- Protein 0 g

Pickles

9. Pickled Garlic scrapes

Preparation time: 5 minutes

Cooking time: 10 minutes

Servings: 3 pint jars

Ingredients:

- 1 lb. garlic scrapes

- 3 tbsp. dill seed

- 1-1/2 tbsp. whole peppercorns 1-1/2 tbsp. whole coriander

- 1-1/2 cups apple cider vinegar

- 1-1/2 cup water

- tbsp. pickling salt

Directions:

1) Trim the scrapes to remove the blossoms and the tough bottom end. Reserve the blossoms for another use.

2) Cut the scrapes to a size that will fit the jars. Pack the scrapes in the jars then add a tablespoon of dill, 1/2 tablespoon peppercorn, and coriander seeds in each jar. You can also attach red pepper flakes for spicy pickles.

3) Merge vinegar, water, and salt in a pot then bring the mixture to boil while stirring until the salt has dissolved.

4) Pour the hot mixture over the garlic scrapes in the jars leaving 1inch headspace.

5) Clear the rim of the jars with a damp cloth then place the lids and rings.

6) Bring the jars in the pressure canner and process for 55 minutes at 10 pounds pressure.

7) Let the canner depressurize to zero before removing the jars. Bring the jars to a rack and let them rest for 24 hours undisturbed.

8) Store the jars in a cool dry place.

Nutrition

- Calories: 20

- Total fat: 0g

- Carbs: 4g

- Protein: 1g

- Sugars: 0g Fiber 0g.

10. Pickled Pullet Eggs

Preparation time: 30 minutes

Cooking time: 20 minutes

Servings: 20 half pint jars

Ingredients:

- 1 white onion, sliced

- 2 Vidalia onions, sliced

- 4-6 fresh garlic cloves, diced

- 2 tbsp. pickling salt

- 1 tbsp. mustard seed

- 1 tbsp. celery seed

- 1 tbsp. pickling spice

- 4-7 chili peppers, fresh

- 3 cups white vinegar

- 1 cup cider vinegar

- 1 cup water

- 24 hard-boiled eggs, peeled (48 pullet eggs)

Directions:

1) Put onions and garlic in a saucepan.

2) Attach the remaining ingredients except eggs and bring them to boil.

3) Place peeled eggs, onions, garlic, and uncut peppers into hot jars, glass, then pour in hot sauce.

4) Place lids immediately. Wipe the jar rims with clean cloth.

5) Process in boiling water in a pressure canner for about 15 minutes.

6) Cool to seal.

Nutrition:

- Calories: 174

- Total fat: 10.8g

- Carbs: 3.6g

- Protein: 13.7g

- Sugars: 1.8g

- Fiber: 0.5g

- Sodium 728mg

11. Canned Spicy Garlic Pickled Carrots

Preparation time: 15 minutes

Cooking time: 25 minutes

Servings: 10 pint jars

Ingredients:

- 8-1/2 cups fresh garden carrots, small and peeled

- 5-1/2 cups white vinegar, distilled

- 2 cups of sugar

- 3 Garlic cloves

- 1 cup water

- 2 tbsp. canning salt

- 3 tbsp. pickling spice

Directions:

1) Wash and peel carrots well.

2) In the meantime, combine vinegar, sugar, garlic, water, and salt in a stockpot, large, bring to a gentle boil for about 3 minutes.

3) Add carrots and boil again. Set heat and simmer for about 10 minutes until carrots are half-cooked.

4) Divide spice among 4 jars then fill the hot jars with hot carrots and leave 1-inch headspace.

5) Scoop pickling liquid into the jars covering the carrots. Leave 1/2inch headspace.

6) Poke a knife through liquid and carrots to remove air bubbles adjusting headspace if necessary.

7) Wipe jar rims with a paper towel then apply 2-pieces canning lids.

8) Process the jars in a pressure canner for about 15 minutes following the manufacturer's guide and according to altitude.

Nutrition

- Calories: 557

- Total fat: 0g

- Carbs: 125g

- Protein: 2g

- Sugars: 112g

- Fiber: 8g

- Sodium: 1389mg

- Potassium: 691mg

12. Sweet and Spicy Pickled Radishes

Preparation time: 30 minutes

Cooking time: 10 minutes

Servings: 6 half pint jars

Ingredients:

- 1-1/2 cups water

- 2 tbsp. canning salt

- 1-1/4 cups white vinegar

- 3/4 cup raw sugar

- 1/4 cup red wine vinegar

- 2 tbsp. mixed peppercorns

- 1 tbsp. mustard seeds

- 1tbsp. red pepper flakes, dried

- 2 lbs. radishes, 1/8 -inch thick

Directions:

1) Combine all ingredients except radishes in a saucepan, medium. Bring to a boil over high-medium heat until salt and sugar dissolves.

2) Place radishes into hot pint jars and leave 1/2 -inch headspace.

3) Scoop hot vinegar mixture into the jars and leave 1/2 -inch headspace then distribute seeds, peppercorns, and flakes among the jars.

4) Clean the jar rims with a cloth. Place lids and rings and tighten to fingertip tight.

5) Process jars in a pressure canner and process for about 10 minutes following manufacturers guide and according to the altitude.

Nutrition

- Calories: 142
- Total fat: 0.9g
- Carbs: 33.2g
- Protein: 1.8g
- Sugars: 28.3g
- Fiber: 3.5g

- Sodium: 1990mg

- Potassium: 456mg

13. **Pickled Bean Salad**

Preparation time: 5 minutes

Cooking time: 10 minutes

Servings: 3 pint jars

Ingredients:

- Kidney beans, canned, drained (1 1/2 cups)

- Green peppers, sliced (1/2 cup)

- Oil (1/4 cup)

- Onion, peeled, sliced thinly (1/2 cup)

- Lemon juice, bottled (1/4 cup)

- Water (1 1/4 cups)

- Yellow/green beans, cut, blanched (1 1/2 cups)

- Garbanzo beans, canned, drained (1 cup)

- Celery, trimmed, sliced thinly (1/2 cup)

- White vinegar, 5% (1/2 cup)

- Sugar (3/4 cup)

- Canning/pickling salt (1/2 teaspoon)

Directions:

1) Wash the fresh beans before snapping the ends off. Cut into two inch pieces and blanch for three minutes. Dip immediately in cold water.

2) Use tap water to rinse the kidney beans, then drain again. Meanwhile, prepare the rest of the vegetables.

3) Fill a pot with the vinegar, water, lemon juice, and sugar. Stir to combine and heat until boiling. Turn the heat off before adding the

4) salt and oil.

5) Stir in the onions, green pepper, celery, and beans; then let the mixture simmer. Put in the refrigerator for twelve to fourteen hours to marinate.

6) Heat the marinated mixture; once boiling, pour into clean and hot Mason jars. Pour the hot liquid into them until the jars are filled up to half-inch from the rims. Get rid of any air bubbles.

7) Clean the rims of the jars before securing on their lids. Process in the pressure canner for fifteen minutes.

Nutrition:

- Calories: 216

- Protein: 1.3g

- Carbs: 56.3g

- Fat: 0.3g

- Sugar: 47.3g

14. Sweet Pickles

Preparation time: 60 minutes (+ 3 hours)

Cooking time: 10 minutes

Servings: 4 pints jars

Ingredients:

- 9 cups sliced pickling cucumbers

- 1 large sweet onion, thinly sliced

- 1/4 cup canning salt

- 12 garlic cloves, crushed

- tsp. celery seed

- tbsp. mustard seed

- 1/2 tsp. whole peppercorns

- 4 bay leaves

- 1 cup sugar

- 1 cup white vinegar

- 1 cup water

- 1/2 cup cider vinegar

Directions:

1) In a nonreactive bowl, combine onion, cucumbers, and salt. Mix well and cover with crushed ice. Let stand for 3 hours. Drain and rinse thoroughly.

2) In a Dutch oven, combine mustard and celery seed, sugar, peppercorns, water, and vinegars. Bring to a boil. Stir until sugar dissolves.

3) Attach cucumber mixture and bring to a boil, stirring occasionally. Simmer for 4-5 minutes, uncovered.

4) Carefully scoop hot mixture into four hot sterilized 1-pint jars, leaving 1/2-inch headspace.

5) Add 1 bay leaf and 3 garlic cloves to each jar. Remove air bubbles and if necessary, adjust headspace by adding hot mixture. Wipe the rims carefully. Place tops on jars and screw on bands until fingertip tight.

6) Bring jars into canner with simmering water, ensuring that they are completely covered with water. Let boil for 10 minutes. Remove jars and cool.

Nutrition:

- Carbohydrates: 8 g

- Fat: 0 g

- Protein: 0 g

- Sodium: 175 mg

- Calories: 35

15. Pickled Green Beans

Preparation time: 20 minutes

Cooking time: 10 minutes

Servings: 4 pint jars

Ingredients:

- 13/4 lbs. fresh green beans

- 1 tsp. cayenne pepper

- 4 garlic cloves, peeled

- 4 tsp. dill seed

- 21/2 cups water

- 21/2 cups white vinegar

- 1/4 cup canning salt

Directions:

1) Pack beans into four hot 1-pint jars to within 1/2-inch of the top.

2) Add dill seed, cayenne, and garlic to jars.

3) In a large saucepan, set the vinegar, water, and salt to a boil.

4) Carefully scoop the hot liquid over beans, leaving 1/4-inch space of the top. Remove air bubbles and if necessary, adjust headspace by adding hot mixture. Wipe the rims carefully. Place tops on jars and screw on bands until fingertip tight.

5) Place jars into canner with boiling water, ensuring that they are completely covered with water. Let boil for 10 minutes. Remove jars and cool.

Nutrition:

- Carbohydrates: 2g

- Fat: 0g

- Protein: 1g

- Sodium: 83mg

- Calories: 9

16.   Christmas Pickled Morsels

Preparation time: 10 minutes

Cooking time: 25 minutes

Servings: 61/2 quarts

Ingredients:

- 1 gallon whole dill pickles

- 3-4 jalapeno peppers, chopped

- 1 tbsp. whole cloves

- 1 lb. whole candied cherries

- 3 jars pearl onions, drained

- 4-5 garlic cloves, minced

- 111/4 cups sugar

- 1 cup white vinegar

- 1 tbsp. mustard seed

- 4-5 whole cinnamon sticks

- 1 tsp. olive oil

Directions:

1) Drain pickles, reserving juice.

2) Cut pickles into 1/2-inch slices and set aside.

3) In a stockpot, combine vinegar, sugar, mustard seed, peppers, cloves, garlic, cinnamon sticks, and pickle juice.

4) Set to cook over medium heat for 10 minutes, stirring until sugar is dissolved.

5) Bring to a boil, and then reduce the heat to a simmer. Cook, uncovered, for 10 minutes.

6) Remove from heat and let cool slightly. Discard cinnamon sticks.

7) In a large bowl, combine onions, cherries, and pickle slices. Pour liquid over pickle mixture. Stir in oil.

8) Refrigerate, covered, for 48 hours, stirring occasionally.

9) Divide mixture among sterilized jars. Store in the refrigerator up to 30 days, covered.

Nutrition:

- Carbohydrates: 25 g

- Fat: 0 g

- Protein: 1 g

- Sodium: 55 mg

- Calories: 99

17.   Pickled Sweet-Sour Squash

Preparation time: 20 minutes

Cooking time: 10 minutes

Servings: 4 pint jars

Ingredients:

- 3 small yellow squash, thinly sliced

- 1 large sweet red pepper, cut into 1/4-inch strips

- 1 medium onion, chopped

- 3/4 cup white vinegar

- 3/4 tsp. mustard seed

- 3/4 tsp. celery seed

- 1/4 tsp. ground mustard

- 1 tbsp. salt

- 1 cup sugar

Directions:

1) Place pepper, squash, and onion in a bowl. Sprinkle with salt and let stand for 1 hour.

2) In a saucepan, combine the remaining ingredients. Bring to a boil.

3) Stir until sugar dissolves.

4) Add vegetables and return to a boil.

5) Remove from heat and cool completely.

6) Set to a covered container and refrigerate for 4 days before serving. May be stored in refrigerator up to 3 weeks.

Nutrition:

- Carbohydrates: 30 g

- Fat: 0 g

- Protein: 1 g

- Sodium: 225 mg

- Calories: 123

18. Giardiniera

Preparation time: 60 minutes

Cooking time: 10 minutes

Servings: 10 pint jars

Ingredients:

- 2 small cauliflowers, broken into florets

- 4 celery ribs, sliced into 1/2-inch slices

- 4 large carrots, sliced

- 11/4 lb. pearl onions, peeled, trimmed

- 4 Serrano peppers, seeded, thinly sliced

- 4 large sweet red peppers, sliced into 1/2-inch strips

- 6 cups white vinegar

- 31/2 cups sugar

- 3 cups water

- 41/2 tsp. canning salt

- 1 tbsp. dried oregano

- 1 tbsp. fennel seed

- 10 bay leaves

- 20 whole peppercorns

- 10 garlic cloves, thinly sliced

Directions:

1) In a stockpot, combine sugar, vinegar, water, oregano, fennel seed and canning salt. Bring to a boil.

2) Add carrots, cauliflower, onions, and celery. Return to a boil.

3) Remove from heat and add peppers.

4) Carefully scoop hot mixture into hot sterilized 1-pint jars, leaving 1/2-inch headspace.

5) Add a few slices of garlic, a bay leaf, and 2 peppercorns to each jar. Remove air bubbles and if necessary, adjust headspace by adding hot mixture. Wipe the rims carefully. Place tops on jars and screw on bands until fingertip tight.

6) Place jars into canner with boiling water, ensuring that they are completely covered with water. Let boil for 10 minutes. Remove jars and cool.

Nutrition:

- Carbohydrates: 3 g

- Fat: 0 g

- Protein: 0 g

- Sodium: 88 mg

- Calories: 15

19. Apple-Walnut Maple Conserve

Preparation time: 55 minutes

Cooking time: 10 minutes

Servings: 8 pint jars

Ingredients:

- 1 ups of chopped peeled Granny Smith apples (about 6 pounds)

- 2cups of sugar

- 2cups of packed brown sugar

- 1cup of maple syrup

- 1tsp. ground cinnamon

- 1tsp. pumpkin pie spice

- 2 cups of finely chopped walnuts, toasted

Directions:

1) Bring apples, sugars, maple syrup, cinnamon, and pie spice to a boil in a stockpot. Cook for 20-30 minutes, uncovered, or until apples are soft and mixture has thickened somewhat. Add the walnuts and mix well.

2) Return to a boil; simmer and stir for another 5 minutes. Carefully pour the heated mixture into 11 half-pint jars, allowing 1/4-inch headspace in every.

3) Remove air bubbles and, if necessary, correct headspace by adding heated mixture. Clean the rims. Screw on bands until fingertip tight; center lids on jars. Set the jars in a canner filled with simmering water, making sure they are completely

covered. Take a boil and reduce to a frying glass for 10 minutes.

4) Remove and chill the jars. Remove them.

Nutrition:

- Carbohydrates: 30 g

- Fat: 0 g

- Protein: 1 g

- Sodium: 225 mg

- Calories: 123

20. Strawberry Pectin Jam

Preparation time: 25 minutes

Cooking time: 10 minutes

Servings: 4 pint jars

Ingredients:

- 2 cups of sliced fresh strawberries

- 1/4 cup lemon juice

- 1 package powdered fruit pectin

- 5 cups of sugar

Directions:

1) Boiling water should be used to rinse five 1-cup of freezer-safe containers and lids. Thoroughly dry. Mix strawberries, lemon juice, and pectin in a large saucepan; bring to a full rolling boil over high heat, stirring frequently.

2) Return to a full rolling boil after adding the sugar. 1 minute longer to boil and stir. Take out the heat and skim wherever excess froth.

3) Fill containers to within 1/2 inch of the tops as soon as possible. Clean the sides of the containers and cover them immediately with lids.

4) Allow yourself to sit for 24 hours at room temperature. Jam is now available for usage. Cool till 3 weeks or freeze for up to one year.

5) Before serving, thaw frozen jam in the refrigerator.

Nutrition:

- Carbohydrates: 2g

- Fat: 0g

- Protein: 1g

- Sodium: 83mg

- Calories: 9

21. Honey-Lavender Peaches

Preparation time: 60 minutes

Cooking time: 5 minutes

Servings: 12 pint jars

Ingredients:

- 15 lb. ripe peaches

- 4 cups water

- 1-3/4 cups honey

- 2/3 cup Riesling

- 1 tbsp. lavender buds, dried

- 1/2 tbsp. salt

- 1 lemon

Directions:

1) Bring a large pot of water into boiling. Cook the peaches, in batches, in the boiling water for 30-60 seconds or until the skin starts to peel.

2) Use a slotted spoon to remove the pitches from the hot water to a large bowl of ice cold water. Remove the peaches from cold water and peel the skin.

3) Cut them into half lengthwise and discard the pits.

4) Make the syrup by combining 4 cups of water, honey, Riesling, lavender buds and salt in a large saucepan. Swirl cook over medium high heat until the honey has all dissolved.

5) Cut 3 inches strips of lemon peel using a vegetable peeler. Reserve the lemon for other use.

6) Pack the peaches in the jars with the cut side down. Add the lemon peel then ladle the syrup evenly among the jars leaving a 1/2 inch headspace.

7) Clean the jar rims, and place the lids and rings on the jars. Transfer the jars to the pressure canner and process at 10 pounds pressure for 70 minutes.

8) Let the canner rest to cool before removing the jars and placing them on a rack to cool.

Nutrition:

- Calories: 77

- Total fat: 0g

- Carbs: 19g

- Protein: 1g

- Sugars: 18g

- Fiber: 2g

- Sodium: 22mg

- Potassium: 213mg

22. Apple Pie Filling

Preparation time: 15 minutes

Cooking time: 25 minutes

Servings: 4 pint jars

Ingredients:

- Lemon juice, bottled (2 tablespoons)

- Sugar, granulated (3/4 cup + 2 tablespoons)

- Apple juice (3/4 cups)

- Cinnamon (1/2 teaspoon)

- Food coloring, yellow (1 drop)

- Apples, fresh, blanched, sliced (3 1/2 cups)

- Liquid pectin (1/4 cup)

- Water, cold (1/2 cup)

- Nutmeg (1/8 teaspoon)

Directions:

1) Choose firm and crispy apples. To add tartness, add a quarter of a cup more lemon juice for every six quarts of sliced apples.

2) Wash the apples before peeling and coring.

3) Slice the apples in half-inch wide slices before submerging in water (1 gallon) mixed with ascorbic acid (1 teaspoon) to keep them from browning before processing in batches.

4) Fill a pot with boiling water (1 gallon). Add the apple slices (6 cups) and boil for one minute, then drain and set aside, covered.

5) Place the sugar, cinnamon, and liquid pectin at the bottom of a large kettle. Fill with apple juice and water, as well as nutmeg and food coloring. Stir to combine before heating over medium-high heat. Cook the mixture until thickened and starting to bubble.

6) Stir in the lemon juice and bring the mixture to a boil for one minute before folding in the drained apple slices. Transfer immediately to clean and hot Mason jars, seeing to it that an inch of headspace remains. Take out any air bubbles.

7) Adjust the lids on the filled jars. Process for twenty-five minutes.

Nutrition:

- Calories 79

- Fat: 0 g

- Carbs: 21 g Protein 0 g

23. Pineapple Peach Spread

Preparation time: 15 minutes

Cooking time: 25 minutes

Servings: 2 pint jars

Ingredients:

- Pineapple, unsweetened, crushed, drained (2 cups)

- Peach pulp, drained (4 cups)

- Sugar (2 cups)

- Lemon juice, bottled (1/4 cup)

Directions:

1) Wash your firm and ripe peaches thoroughly.

2) Drain the peaches before peeling and discarding the pits.

3) Use a coarse blade to grind the peach flesh, then add to a saucepan (2-quart).

4) Heat over medium-low and allow the peaches to release their juices as you constantly stir. When the peaches are tender, transfer them to a strainer or jelly bag lined with cheesecloth (4 layers). Let the juices drip into a bowl for about fifteen minutes (reserve for making jelly).

5) Take four cups of the drained peach pulp and add to a saucepan (4quart). Mix with lemon juice, sugar (2 cups), and pineapple. Heat over medium and boil for about ten to fifteen minutes or until thickened, stirring constantly to keep from sticking to the pan.

6) Pour the spread into clean and hot Mason jars. Wipe the rims with paper towels before fitting with the lids.

7) Process your canned spread in the pressure canner for fifteen minutes (if using half-pint jars) or twenty minutes (if using quart jars).

Nutrition:

- Calories: 262

- Total: fat 0g

- Carbs: 67g

- Protein: 1g

- Sugars: 55g Fiber: 6g

24. Fresh Berries

Preparation time: 15 minutes

Cooking time: 25 minutes

Servings: 4 pint jars

Ingredients:

- 1 gallon (5.5 pounds) fresh berries

- 7 cups distilled or filtered water

- 7 tablespoons lemon juice

Directions:

1) Pour some lemon juice into the jar using the following ratio: 1 tablespoon for every pint-sized jar or 2 tablespoons for every quart-sized jar.

2) Add the berries to the jar. You should also discard mushy or soft berries.

3) Set the jars with water, leaving about 1/2-inch of space at the top.

4) Add the lids. Use the water bath canning method (30 minutes for quart-sized jars or 15 minutes for pint-sized jars) to seal the preserve the berries.

Nutrition:

- Carbohydrates: 3 g

- Fat: 0 g

- Protein: 1 g

- Sodium: 11 mg Calories: 14

25. Berry Syrup

Preparation time: 15 minutes

Cooking time: 10 minutes

Servings: 2 pint jars

Ingredients:

- Mixed berries, fresh/frozen (6 1/2 cups)

- Sugar (6 3/4 cups)

Directions:

1) Wash the mixed berries (blueberries, raspberries, strawberries) before capping, stemming, and crushing in the saucepan.

2) Set the mixture to a boil, then simmer for five to ten minutes or until softened.

3) Pass the hot berries through a colander to strain. Collect the juice through two pieces of clean cheesecloth; throw away the dry pulp.

4) Pour the collected juice (about four and a half to five cups) into a large saucepan. Add the sugar and stir to combine. Heat until boiling, then simmer for one minute.

5) Turn the heat off and spoon off any foam forming on top of the syrup. Pour into clean and hot Mason jars, making sure each jar is filled to 1/2-inch from the top.

6) Remove air bubbles and wipe-clean the rims of the jars before securing their lids. Place in the pressure canner to process for ten minutes.

Nutrition:

- Calories 25

- Fat: 0 g

- Carbs: 6 g

- Protein 0 g

Vegetables

26. Tomato with Hot Pepper

Preparation time: 13 minutes

Cooking time: 45 minutes

Servings: 1 pint jars

Ingredients:

- 1 ounds (5.4 kg) of tomatoes, peeled and cut into chunks

- 3bell peppers, diced

- 1large onion, diced

- 2 pounds (907 g) diced hot peppers

- 1 cup white vinegar

- 1/4 cup sugar

- 4 tablespoons chili powder

- 2 tablespoons canning salt

- 1 tablespoon lime juice per jar

Directions:

1) Set all of the ingredients except for the lime juice into a large stockpot and stir to combine everything.

2) Place the mixture to a simmer, and allow it to cook uncovered for 45 minutes to reduce the liquid and meld the delicious flavors.

3) Attach a tablespoon of lime juice to each pint jar then ladle in the super-yummy mixture, leaving 1/2 inch of headspace.

4) Pop the lids on and then process this in a water bath canner for 15 minutes, adjusting for altitude.

Nutrition:

- Calories: 171

- Total fat: 0g

- Carbs: 44g,

- Protein: 0g

- Sugars: 36g

- Fiber: 2g

- Sodium: 52mg

- Potassium: 146mg

27. Crushed Tomato

Preparation time: 18 minutes

Cooking time: 12 minutes

Servings: 7 pint jars

Ingredients:

- 22 pounds (10 kg) of tomatoes

- Bottled lemon juice or citric acid

- 1 teaspoon of salt

Directions:

1) Clean the tomatoes and dip in boiling water for 30 to 60 seconds or until skins split. Then set in cold water, slip off skins, and remove cores.

2) Set off any bruised or discolored portions and quarter. Heat 1/6 of the quarters quickly in a large pot, crushing them.

3) Continue heating the tomatoes, swirling to prevent burning. The rest of the tomatoes do not need to be smashed. They will soften with heating and stirring.

4) Continue until all tomatoes are attached. Then boil gently 5 minutes. Attach bottled lemon juice or citric acid to jars.

5) Attach 1 teaspoon of salt per quart to the jars, if desired.

6) Set hot jars immediately with hot tomatoes, leaving 1/2-inch headspace.

7) Detach air bubbles and adjust headspace if needed.

8) Clean rims of jars with a dampened clean paper towel. Adjust lids and process.

Nutrition:

- Calories: 49 Fat: 0.2g

- Carbs: 8.7g,

- Protein: 3.6g Sugars: 4.9g

28. Quick Pickled Red Onions

Preparation time: 30 minutes

Cooking time: 15 minutes

Servings: 4 pint jars

Ingredients:

- 2 large red onions (sliced thinly)

- 2 cups of 5% white vinegar (Please read the vinegar bottle and make sure it says 5%)

- 1 cup of water

- 2 tbsp. white sugar (or honey)

- 1 tsp. pickling spice (you can buy Ball Pickling Spice at Walmart and some grocery stores)

- 1 tbsp. pickling salt Please buy pickling salt only

Directions:

1) Spiralize the vegetables using a sharp knife or a vegetable spiralizer. Thinly slice the red onion. In every jar, put 1 tsp. of pickling spice. Fill every canning jar or a lidded recycling jar halfway with chopped onions.

2) Combine the white vinegar, water, sugar, and pickling salt in a mixing bowl. in a medium non-reactive stainless steel or stainless steel saucepan Stir in the sugar and salt until they are completely dissolved. Then bring to a boil the salt components remove from the heat. Remove from the heat. Into the jar, ladle the hot brine over the cut onions.

3) Push the onions down into the brine with a canning bubbler or a plastic spoon. When the onions have settled, you can add more onion slices to the jar. Put a flat canned deck on top the jar after wiping the rim with a paper towel. Attach a canning lid band. Allow for an hour to cool to room temperature.

4) Refrigerate and keep for up to four months in the refrigerator. This recipe makes 3 half-pint jars of pickled onions.

Nutrition:

- Carbohydrates: 1 g

- Fat: 0 g

- Protein: 1 g

- Sodium: 727 mg

- Calories: 4

29. Kale

Preparation time: 35 minutes

Cooking time: 10 minutes

Servings: 5 pint jars

Ingredients:

- 10 lb. Kale water

Directions:

1) Chop the kale into bite-size pieces then remove all the hard stems and yellow parts of the kale.

2) Clean the kale to remove any dirt then add it to the stockpot. Cover the kale with water.

3) Bring the water to boil until the kale has wilted nicely.

4) Use a slotted spoon to full the jars with kale then add 1/2 tablespoon salt in each jar. Add the cooking liquid and leave a 1inch headspace.

5) Remove any air bubble and add more cooking liquid if necessary. Clean the rims and place the lids and rings on the jars.

6) Process the jars at 10-11 pounds of pressure for 70 minutes. Set off the heat and let the canner cool before using a jar lifer to remove the jars.

7) Let rest for 24 hours undisturbed before storing them in a cool dry place.

Nutrition:

- Calories: 85

- Total fat: 0.5g

- Carbs: 6.7g

- Protein: 2.2g

- Sugars: 0g

- Fiber: 1.3g

- Sodium: 28.8mg

- Potassium: 299mg

30. Turnips

Preparation time: 35 minutes

Cooking time: 10 minutes

Servings: 12 pint jars

Ingredients:

- 10 lb. turnips water

Directions:

1) Peel the turnips then dice them into small pieces

2) Add the turnips in a stockpot and add cold water until just covered.

3) Drain the water to get lid of dirt and debris.

4) Cover with water once more and bring them to boil over mediumhigh heat. Reduce heat and let simmer for 5 minutes.

5) Use a slotted spoon to set the hot turnips in sterilized jars. Fill the jar with the cooking liquid leaving 1-inch headspace. Add a half tablespoon of pickling salt.

6) Remove any air bubble and add the cooking liquid if necessary. Wipe the pint jars and place the lids and rings.

7) Load the jars into the pressure canner and process at 10 pounds for 30 minutes.

8) Allow the canner to depressurize to zero before removing the jars.

Nutrition:

- Calories: 36.4

- Total fat: 0.13g

- Carbs: 8.36g

- Protein: 1.17g

- Sugars: 1g

- Fiber: 2.34g

- Sodium: 87.1mg

31. Mushroom

Preparation time: 25 minutes

Cooking time: 15 minutes

Servings: 4 pint jars

Ingredients:

- 4 pounds of mushrooms

- 2 1/2 pounds of lettuce or cabbage

- 2 pounds of carrots

- 1 pound of onions

Directions:

1) Clean the mushrooms.

2) Slice all of the ingredients and transfer them to a pan. Fry them together in vegetable oil over low heat for approximately an hour.

3) Add salt to taste.

4) Set into jars while still hot and seal. Store refrigerated. It can be served both hot and cold.

Nutrition:

- Calories: 8

- Total fat: 0.1g

- Carbs: 1.5g

- Protein: 0.6g

- Sugars: 0.4g Fiber: 0.6g

32. Easy Cabbage Salads

Preparation time: 25 minutes

Cooking time: 10 minutes

Servings: 2 pint jars

Ingredients:

- 2 pounds of carrots 1 large garlic clove

- 4-5 tablespoons of 9% vinegar

- 3 tablespoons of sugar

- 1/2 cup of vegetable oil

- 1 teaspoon of ground black pepper a pinch of coriander

Directions:

1) Grate carrots (thin and long).

2) Mince garlic.

3) Attach the remaining ingredients and mix everything together.

4) Store refrigerated.

Nutrition:

- Calories 149

- Fat: 0.4 g

- Carbs: 37.7 g Protein 1.3 g

33. Stewed Tomatoes and Vegetables

Preparation time: 75 minutes

Cooking time: 30 minutes

Servings: 16 pint jars

Ingredients:

- 8 pounds tomatoes

- 1large celery, chopped

- 1large yellow onion, peeled and chopped

- 1tablespoon sugar

- 2 teaspoons salt

- Juice from 1 lemon

Directions:

1) Sterilize the bottles. Allow the bottles to cool.

2) Set the tomatoes in hot water and peel off the skin. Chop the tomatoes and set aside.

3) Bring all ingredients in a saucepan and bring to a boil for 20 minutes,

4) Turn off the heat and allow the mixture to slightly cool.

5) Transfer the mixture to sterilized bottles and remove the air bubbles.

6) Close the lid and place band on tightening to finger tight. Place the jars and process for 25 minutes.

Nutrition:

- Calories: 52

- Protein: 2.1g

- Carbs: 10.1g

- Fat: 1.1g

- Sugar: 6.8g

34. Almond Apricot Jam

Preparation time: 10 minutes

Cooking time: 30 minutes

Servings: 2 pint jars

Ingredients:

- 2 -1/2 cups unsweetened apple juice

- 1 cup diced dried apricots (8 oz.)

- 1/4 to 1/2 tsp. almond extract

- 1/4 tsp. ground cinnamon

Directions:

1) Boil apricots and apple juice in a saucepan. Lower the heat; simmer till apricots are tender or for 20-25 minutes while

uncovering. Take off the heat; mash to preferred consistency. Mix in cinnamon and almond extract; put into a pint jar and cover. Refrigerate for 3 weeks maximum.

Nutrition:

- Calories: 37

- Protein: 1.9g

- Carbs: 7.4g

- Fat: 0.8g

- Sugar: 1.3g

Salsa and Sauces

35. Tangy Cranberry Sauce

Preparation time: 10 minutes

Cooking time: 15 minutes

Servings: 6 pint jars

Ingredients:

- 4 (12-ounces / 340-g) bags fresh cranberries (8 cups)

- 2 cups sugar

- 2 cups water

- 2 cups bottled orange juice

- 2 large oranges, peeled, pith removed, seeded, and chopped

- 1/2 teaspoon ground allspice (optional)

- 1/2 teaspoon ground cloves (optional)

Directions:

1) In a smaller pot, attach lids and rings, 1 tbsp. distilled white vinegar, and water to cover. Boil for 5 minutes, then detach from heat.

2) In a large pot, combine the cranberries, sugar, water, orange juice, oranges, allspice, and cloves. Set to a boil over medium-high heat, stirring often. Set the heat to low and simmer for 15 minutes. Stir often, muddling the orange pieces with your spoon. Remove from heat.

3) Set the hot jars on a cutting board. Using a funnel, ladle the hot sauce into the jars, leaving a 1/2-inch headspace. Detach any air bubbles and add additional sauce if necessary to maintain the 1/2inch headspace.

4) Clean the jar with a warm washcloth dipped in distilled white vinegar. Set a lid and ring on each jar and hand-tighten.

5) Bring the jars in the water bather, ensuring each jar is covered by at least 1 inch of water. Attach 2 tablespoons distilled white vinegar to the water and turn the heat to high. Set the canner to a boil and process both quarts and pints for 15 minutes. When processed, wait 5 minutes before removing the jars from the canner.

Nutrition:

- Calories 25

- Fat: 0 g

- Carbs: 6 g

- Protein 0 g

36. Spaghetti Sauce with Tomato

Preparation time: 20 minutes

Cooking time: 2-3 hours minutes

Servings: 6 pint jars

Ingredients:

- 3 o 35 pounds (14-16 kg) fresh canning tomatoes

- 1tablespoon olive oil

- 1medium onion, finely chopped

- 2 cloves garlic, minced

- 2 bay leaves

- 2 tablespoons garlic powder

- 1 teaspoon parsley flakes

- 1 teaspoon Italian seasoning

- 1 teaspoon dried oregano

- 1 teaspoon dried basil

- 1 teaspoon dried summer savory

- 1 teaspoon dried tarragon

- 1 teaspoon white pepper

- 1tablespoon salt

- 1teaspoon onion powder

- 2 tablespoons organic or non-GMO granulated sugar

- 2 tablespoons lemon juice per jar

Directions:

1) Wash tomatoes and cut off any bruised or damaged areas. Blanch

2) the tomatoes. This process is easily done in stages and requires a large pot of boiling water and another pot or bowl of ice water. Set a pot of water to a boil and add in tomatoes once the pot begins to boil. Set the timer for 1 minute. Use a slotted spoon to carefully detach the tomatoes from the hot water and put them in the ice bath. You should see the tomato skins split while in the boiling water or once added to the ice bath. Redo this process until all the tomatoes are blanched. This method will make removing the skins from the tomatoes

a quick job, as the skin will easily fall off the fruit with a little rub of the fingers. Then, core the tomatoes and cut them into quarters.

3) Once all tomatoes are blanched, peeled, cored, and cut, add them to a large (at least 7 quarts) pot. Using a hand blender, break down the tomatoes into the consistency you want your sauce to have.

4) In a medium frying pan, warmth the olive oil and sauté the onion and garlic. Once the onion is translucent, it's done; this typically takes about 5 minutes. Add mixture to the tomatoes and add in all the seasonings. Mix well and heat the pot to a medium-high simmer. The sauce will need to cook for 2 to 3 hours to thicken. It must be stirred occasionally to avoid burning.

5) Once the sauce has thickened, detach the bay leaves. Prepare the quart jars with 2 tablespoons of lemon juice per jar. This will add acidity to the sauce that will keep it from growing unsafe bacteria.

6) Ladle the sauce into warm, prepared jars. Use a funnel to safely transfer the sauce, leaving 1/2 inch of headspace. Clean the jars with a dampened, clean, lint-free cloth or paper towel and again with a dry towel. Place canning lid on the jar and twist the canning ring on until it's just-snug on the jar. Set the jars into the canning pot, and make sure the jars are covered

by at least 1 inch of water. Set the lid on the canning pot and once the water bath reaches a rolling boil, set the timer and process in the water bath for 40 minutes. Carefully remove jars from the water bath with canning tongs and place the jars on a towel-lined surface for 12 to 24 hours without touching.

Nutrition:

- Calories: 314

- Protein: 0.9 g

- Carbs: 81.1 g

- Fat: 0.2 g

- Sugar: 77.6g

37. Autumn Pepper Salsa

Preparation time: 1 hour 20 minutes

Cooking time: 20 minutes

Servings: 8 half-pints

Ingredients:

- 3 lbs. sweet red peppers, seeded, coarsely chopped

- 6 jalapeno peppers, seeded, coarsely chopped

- 11/4 lbs. Granny Smith apples, peeled, cut into 1-inch. pieces

- 1 lb. pears, peeled, cut into 1-inch pieces

- 1 medium onion, cut into 1-inch pieces

- 3/4 tsp. fennel seed

- 3 tbsp. canning salt

- cups white vinegar

- 2 cups sugar

- 1 cup packed brown sugar

Directions:

1) Process peppers, apples, pears and onion in a food processor until finely chopped. et to a bowl and sprinkle with salt and toss.

2) Allow to stand 6 hours.

3) Drain well.

4) In a Dutch oven, combine pepper mixture, sugars, fennel seed, and vinegar. Bring to a boil, then let parboil, uncovered, 40-45 minutes until slightly thickened.

5) Carefully scoop hot mixture into hot sterilized half-pint jars, leaving 1/2-inch headspace. Remove air bubbles and if necessary, adjust headspace by adding hot mixture. Wipe the

rims carefully. Place tops on jars and screw on bands until fingertip tight.

6) Place jars into canner with boiling water, ensuring that they are completely covered with water. Let boil; for 20 minutes. Remove jars and cool.

Nutrition:

- Carbohydrates: 3 g

- Fat: 0 g

- Protein: 0 g

- Sodium: 4 mg

- Calories: 13

38. Pear Sauce

Preparation time: 2 hours 45 minutes

Cooking time: 20 minutes

Servings: 5 pints

Ingredients:

- 14-16 pears (if using small pears, you may want to include up to 20)

- Cinnamon to taste (about 1/2 teaspoon per jar); this is an optional ingredient

Directions:

1) To prepare the pear sauce, you'll need large spoons and ladles, jar lifters, and a water bath canner. Pears should be scrubbed and washed thoroughly with a scrub and cold water. Remove any labels, stickers, and then peel using a paring knife or peeler. This process is optional, and you may decide to leave the peel intact, as it can be removed later with a sieve, along with the stems and seeds.

2) Chop the pears with a knife by hand or use a core-cutting device that simultaneously slices the pears into pieces while taking out the seeds inside. A food mill can also remove the seeds so that you do

3) not have to peel manually.

4) Place the pears in a large cooking pot and cover with water, then cover and heat on high, bringing the contents to a boil. Once the boiling point is reached, reduce the heat to medium-high and continue to cook for another 10-15 minutes or until the pears are tender. They should be mushy enough to mash through a sieve and remove any excess seeds, peeling, and stems not removed prior to this step. Push the pears through a sieve and into a large bowl that's sterilized.

5) Set the jars by washing them in warm water and soap, then set them in boiling water for at least 10 minutes, along with

the lids. Use a jar lifter to remove them and place on a cloth, then gently scoop the pear sauce in each jar, leaving 1/2 inch at the top. Fasten the lids on each jar and prepare the water bath.

6) Add the filled jars into a water bath canner and cover with water to one inch above each. Bring to a boil and cover, then process for about 10-12 minutes. Remove with a jar lifter and set on a wire rack or cloth on the countertop. Leave the pear sauce overnight to cool, then store in a pantry or cold, dark area for up to one year.

Nutrition:

- Calories 79

- Fat: 0 g

- Carbs: 21 g

- Protein 0 g

39. Apple Sauce

Preparation time: 45 minutes

Cooking time: 20 minutes

Servings: 2 pint jars Ingredients:

Ingredients:

- Apples (about 20 in total, or three pounds)

- Water

- Lemon juice, bottled (optional)

- Sugar (optional)

- Cinnamon (optional)

Directions:

1) Pour water and lemon juice into a large cooking pot. The amount of water should cover about 1/3 of the interior. Ascorbic acid can be used in place of lemon juice, if available, or this ingredient can be omitted altogether. Peel, core, and slice the apples, removing all the seeds. As each apple is peeled, set inside the water so that it does not brown. Rinse each apple before adding to the cooking pot. Add any sugar and cinnamon as desired, or wait to add these ingredients later, if you're uncertain at this point.

2) Bring the apples to a boil, and stir regularly, then reduce the heat to a simmer and cook for five minutes for about 30 minutes, or until all the apples are tender or soft. Some apples, depending on the variety, can soften while others need more time. Once they soften, apples will be easy to break down in a food mill or sieve, then set in a blender or food processor. If you prefer a chunky texture, skip the blender and mash lightly until you achieve the desired consistency.

3) Set the sauce to the pot and add the sugar and cinnamon, then cook and bring back to a boil. Transfer the apple sauce into sterilized jars and add a bit of lemon juice, if desired. Give 1/2 inch of space at the top of each jar. Wipe the rims of each jar and place the lids on tightly. Set the jars in the water bath canner or a pressure canner for about 8-10 minutes, then detach from heat and allow to cool on a wire rack or cloth on the countertop. Set the jars in cool place or the pantry for up to one year.

Nutrition:

- Calories: 36.4

- Total fat: 0.13g

- Carbs: 8.36g

- Protein: 1.17g

- Sugars: 1g

- Fiber: 2.34g

- Sodium: 87.1mg

40. Mango Salsa

Preparation time: 45 minutes

Cooking time: 20 minutes

Servings: 2 pint jars

Ingredients:

- 6 cups of mangoes, diced thinly

- Brown sugar, 1 cup

- Garlic cloves, 2

- 1/2 cup of water

- Medium red onion, finely diced

- Red bell pepper, sliced finely and seeds removed about 1 1/2 cups

- Red pepper flakes, 1/2 teaspoon

- Fresh cilantro, two teaspoons

- Chopped fresh ginger, two teaspoons

- Vinegar (white or cider), about one 1/4 cups

Directions:

1) In a large cooking pot, toss in the ingredients and bring them to a boil over a high temperature. Stir regularly until the sugar

dissolves. Set the temperature in low to a simmer and continue cooking for about five minutes. Scoop the mixture with a slotted spoon and transfer into all the jars, leaving about 1/2 inch at the top of each. Add a bit of liquid to the top, not including the 1/2 inch of space. If there isn't enough room at the top, reduce slightly with a smaller spoon until this is achieved.

2) Wipe the rim and outside of the jars with a clean towel with a small amount of vinegar. Affix the lids and process the jars in boiling water (water bath canner) for about 15-17 minutes. If the size of the jars is smaller, such as a half pint, then process for about 10 minutes.

Nutrition:

- Calories: 49 Fat: 0.2g

- Carbs: 8.7g,

- Protein: 3.6g

- Sugars: 4.9g

41. Fresh Green Salsa

Preparation time: 10 minutes

Cooking time: 30 minutes

Servings: 12 pint jars

Ingredients:

- 2 jalapeno peppers, diced

- 6green onions, sliced

- 7 cups tomatoes, diced

- 4 cloves garlic, minced

- 2 tablespoons minced cilantro

- 4 drops hot pepper sauce

- 2 tablespoons lime juice

- 1/2 cup vinegar

- 2 teaspoons salt

Directions:

1) 1. Merge all ingredients in a pan; set to a boil and then simmer for about 15 minutes. ladle in sterile jars and seal. Bring in a hot water bath for about 15 minutes and then let cool before storing in the fridge.

Nutrition:

- Calories: 5

- Total Fat: 0 g

- Carbs: 0.4 g

- Sugars: 0.6 g

- Protein: 0.2 g

42. Corn, Avocado and Tomato Salsa

Preparation time: 30 minutes

Cooking time: 0 minutes

Servings: 16 pint jars

Ingredients:

- 1 avocados - peeled, pitted and diced

- 1 1/2 cups diced tomatoes

- 1/2 cup sliced black olives

- 1 1/2 cups whole kernel corn

- 11/2 teaspoons minced jalapeno pepper

- 3/4 cup diced red onion

- 1 red bell pepper, diced

- 2 tablespoons fresh lime juice

- 2 tablespoons olive oil

- 1 teaspoon salt

Directions:

1) In a large bowl, combine together onion, tomatoes, olives, corn, jalapeno and red pepper; fold in avocado, lime juice, olive oil and salt. Transfer an airtight can and refrigerate until chilled before serving.

Nutrition:

- Calories: 68

- Total Fat: 4.5 g

- Carbs: 7.1 g

- Sugars: 1.8 g

- Protein: 1.1 g

Marmalades

43. Lemon Honey Marmalade

Preparation Time: 10 minutes

Cooking Time: 40 minutes

Servings: 12 pint jars

Ingredients:

- 8 cups lemons, chopped

- 6 oz. liquid pectin

- 1 1/2 cups water

- 4 cups sugar

- 2 cups honey

Directions:

1) Add lemons, sugar, water, and honey in a saucepan and bring to boil over medium heat.

2) Reduce heat and simmer for 30 minutes.

3) Add pectin and boil for 5 minutes. Stir constantly.

4) Remove pan from heat. Ladle the marmalade into the jars. Leave 1/2-inch headspace. Remove air bubbles.

5) Secure jars with lids and process in a boiling water bath for 10 minutes.

6) Remove jars from the water bath and let it cool completely.

7) Check seals of jars. Label and store.

Nutrition:

- Calories 468

- Fat 0.4 g

- Carbohydrates 127.5 g

- Sugar 116.6 g

- Protein 1.7 g

- Cholesterol 0 mg

44. Strawberry Marmalade

Preparation Time: 10 minutes

Cooking Time: 20 minutes

Servings: 12 pint jars

Ingredients:

- 4 cups strawberries, crushed

- 6 cups sugar

- 6 tbsp. pectin

- 1 lemon

Directions:

1) Cut lemon peel and reserved lemon juice and pulp. Add lemon peel in a small pot with water and boil for 5 minutes. Drain lemon peels.

2) Add strawberries, sugar, pectin, lemon peel, lemon juice, and lemon pulp into the large stockpot. Stir well and bring to boil. Stir until sugar is dissolved.

3) Set heat to high and boil for 1 minute. Stir constantly.

4) Remove pot from heat.

5) Ladle the marmalade into the clean and hot jars. Leave 1/2-inch headspace. Remove air bubbles.

6) Secure jars with lids and process in a boiling water bath for 10 minutes.

7) Remove jars from the water bath and let it cool completely.

8) Check seals of jars. Label and store.

Nutrition:

- Calories 396

- Fat 0.1 g

- Carbohydrates 104 g

- Sugar 102 g

- Protein 0.3 g

- Cholesterol 0 mg

45. Onion Marmalade

Preparation Time: 10 minutes

Cooking Time: 25 minutes

Servings: 4 pint jars

Ingredients:

- 2 large onions, sliced

- 1 tbsp. red wine vinegar

- 1/3 cup red wine

- 1 tsp. sugar

- 1/4 cup olive oil Pinch of salt

Directions:

1) Warmth oil in a small saucepan over medium heat.

2) Add onion and cook for 10-15 minutes or until onion is softened.

3) Add sugar and cook for 5 minutes. Attach wine and cook until wine is reduced.

4) Remove pan from heat. Add vinegar and salt and mix well.

5) Pour marmalade in a clean jar. Secure jar with lid and store in the refrigerator.

Nutrition:

- Calories 159

- Fat 12.7 g

- Carbohydrates 8.6 g

- Sugar 4.4 g

- Protein 0.8 g

- Cholesterol 0 mg

46. Pear Marmalade

Preparation Time: 10 minutes

Cooking Time: 10 minutes

Servings: 12 pint jars

Ingredients:

- 4 medium ripe pears, peeled and quartered

- 5 1/2 cups sugar

- 1.75oz. pectin

- 1 tbsp. orange zest, grated

- 2 tbsp. lemon juice

- 1/2 cup orange juice

- 8oz. crushed pineapple

Directions:

1) Add pears into the food processor and process until pureed.

2) Add pear puree, pectin, orange zest, lemon juice, orange juice, and pineapple into the saucepan and bring to boil over high heat. Stir constantly.

3) Add sugar and stir well and boil for 1 minute. Stir constantly.

4) Remove pot from heat and let it cool completely.

5) Pour marmalade in a clean jar. Secure jar with lid and store in the refrigerator.

Nutrition:

- Calories 393

- Fat 0.1 g

- Carbohydrates 104.1 g

- Sugar 99.8 g

- Protein 0.4 g

- Cholesterol 0 mg

47. Tangy Navel Orange Marmalade

Preparation Time: 10 minutes

Cooking Time: 15 minutes

Servings: 3 pint jars

Ingredients:

- Water 8 tbs.

- Sugar 2 cup

- Navel oranges, medium size – 4

Directions:

1) At first, take the oranges, cut ends and make pieces from it.

2) After that, detach it from the heat; let it cool down.

3) Then take your food processor; add the pieces into it and thoroughly process them.

4) Then take the pre-sterilized jars; place the marmalade mixture into the jars.

5) To make the marmalade, take a saucepan of medium size; mix in the water, sugar, and orange.

6) Keep 1/2" margin from the top.

7) 6. Use a damp cloth to clean jar rims; then close them with the lid and band. Keep the heat on medium setting; let the mixture heat for about 12-15 minutes. Place them to refrigerate and enjoy it chilled!

Nutrition:

- Carbohydrates: 3 g

- Fat: 0 g

- Protein: 0 g

- Sodium: 182 mg

- Calories: 14

48.   Blueberry Orange Marmalade

Preparation Time: 15 minutes

Cooking Time: 25 minutes

Servings: 3 pint jars

Ingredients:

- 1/2 cup water

- 1/8 teaspoon baking soda

- 1 small orange, peeled and chopped

- 1small lemon, peeled and chopped

- 2 cups blueberries, crushed

- 21/2 cups sugar

- 1/2 (6-ounce) package liquid fruit pectin

Directions:

1) In a saucepan or cooking pot, merge the water and baking soda.

2) Boil the mixture; cook for about 10 minutes over low heat. Stir continually to prevent scorching.

3) Add the sugar, berries, lemon and orange.

4) Boil the mixture; cook for about 5 minutes over medium-low heat. Stir continually to prevent scorching.

5) Mix in the pectin and simmer for about 1 minutes over mediumlow heat until firm and thick. Stir continually to prevent scorching.

6) Spill the hot mixture into pre-sterilized jars directly or with a jar funnel. Keep headspace of 1/4 inch from the jar top.

7) To detach tiny air bubbles, insert a nonmetallic spatula and stir the mixture gently.

8) Clean the sealing edges with a damp cloth. Secure the jars with the lids and adjust the bands/rings to seal and prevent any leakage.

9) Set the jars in a hot water bath for 10 minutes.

10) Set the jars in a cool, dry and dark place. Allow them to cool down completely.

11) Store in your refrigerator and use within 10 days.

Nutrition:

- Calories 393

- Fat 0.1 g

- Carbohydrates 104.1 g

- Sugar 99.8 g

- Protein 0.4 g

- Cholesterol 0 mg

49. **Kumquats Marmalade**

Preparation Time: 5 minutes

Cooking Time: 30 minutes

Servings: 2 pint jars

Ingredients:

- 1/2 cup sugar

- 2 cups kumquats, chopped

- 1/2 cup water

- Pinch of ground cinnamon and ground cardamom

Directions:

1) In a deep saucepan, combine the sugar, spices and kumquats.

2) Boil the mixture till thermometer reads 220F; cook for about 12– 15 minutes over medium heat. Stir continually to prevent scorching.

3) Add water and combine.

4) Boil the mixture 220F; cook for about 15 minutes over medium heat until firm and thick. Swirl continually to prevent scorching.

5) Spill the hot mixture into pre-sterilized jars directly or with a jar funnel. Keep headspace of 1/4 inch from the jar top.

6) To detach tiny air bubbles, insert a nonmetallic spatula and stir the mixture gently.

7) Clean the sealing edges with a damp cloth. Secure the jars with the lids and adjust the bands/rings to seal and prevent any leakage.

8) Set the jars in a cool, dry and dark place. Allow them to cool down completely.

9) Store in your refrigerator and use within 10 days.

Nutrition:

- Carbohydrates: 1 g

- Fat: 0 g

- Protein: 0 g

- Sodium: 30 mg

- Calories: 3

50. Orange Marmalade

Preparation Time: 15 minutes

Cooking Time: 15 minutes

Servings: 2 pint jars

Ingredients:

- 1/2 cup water

- 4 medium navel oranges, peeled and cut into small pieces

- 2 cups sugar

Directions

1) Add the orange pieces to a blender or food processor. Blend well.

2) In a deep saucepan, combine the orange mixture, water and sugar.

3) Set the mixture till thermometer reads 220F; cook for about 12–15 minutes over medium heat until firm and thick. Stir continually to prevent scorching.

4) Spill the hot mixture into pre-sterilized jars directly or with a jar funnel. Keep headspace of 1/4 inch from the jar top.

5) To detach tiny air bubbles, insert a nonmetallic spatula and stir the mixture gently.

6) Clean the sealing edges with a damp cloth. Secure the jars with the lids and adjust the bands/rings to seal and prevent any leakage.

7) Set the jars in a cool, dry and dark place. Allow them to cool down completely.

8) Store in your refrigerator and use within 10 days.

Nutrition:

- Carbohydrates: 1 g

- Fat: 0 g

- Protein: 1 g

- Sodium: 727 mg

- Calories: 4g

51. Onion Garlic Marmalade

Preparation Time: 5 minutes

Cooking Time: 40 minutes

Servings: 3 pint jars

Ingredients:

- 4-5 cups sweet onion, thinly sliced

- 1tablespoon red wine vinegar

- 11/2 tablespoons brown sugar

- 1/2 tablespoon butter

- 1/2 teaspoon salt

- 1 garlic cloves, minced

- 1/8 teaspoon ground black pepper

Directions:

1) In a deep saucepan or cooking pot, merge the sugar, onion and garlic.

2) Boil the mixture; cook for about 25-30 minutes over medium heat.

3) Stir continually to prevent scorching.

4) Mix in the vinegar, butter, salt and pepper.

5) Set the mixture till thermometer reads 220°F; cook for about 10– 12 minutes over medium heat until firm and thick. Stir continually to prevent scorching.

6) Spill the hot mixture into pre-sterilized jars directly or with a jar funnel. Keep headspace of 1/4 inch from the jar top.

7) To detach tiny air bubbles, insert a nonmetallic spatula and stir the mixture gently.

8) Clean the sealing edges with a damp cloth. Secure the jars with the lids and adjust the bands/rings to seal and prevent any leakage.

9) Set the jars in a cool, dry and dark place. Allow them to cool down completely.

10) Store in your refrigerator and use within 10 days.

Nutrition:

- Calories 43

- Fat 0 g

- Carbohydrates 11.3 g

- Sugar 11 g

- Protein 0.1 g

- Cholesterol 0 mg

52. Three-Fruit Marmalade

Preparation Time: 15 Minutes

Cooking Time: 15 Minutes

Servings: 8 Half-Pints

Ingredients:

- 2 Cups chopped peeled fresh peaches

- Cups sugar

- 1Medium orange

- 1Package (1 3/4 ounces) powdered fruit pectin

- 2 Cups chopped peeled fresh pears

Directions:

1) Grate the orange peel. Peel and section the orange fruit. Put the orange sections and peel in a Dutch oven.

2) Stir in pears, peaches and add the pectin; bring it to a full boil on high heat.

3) Stir often and add the sugar. Return to a complete rolling boil, boil again and stir for one minute.

4) Remove from the burner, skimming off the foam.

5) Ladle the hot marmalade into eight sterilized half-pint jars with one-fourth inch headspace.

6) With a plastic spoon, remove the air bubbles, adjusting headspace by pouring the hot mixture if desired.

7) Wipe the rims with cloth, center the lids on the jars and screw on band up to fingertip tight.

8) Place the jars in the canner with enough simmering water to cover the entire jars.

9) Bring water to a full rolling boil and process for ten minutes. Detach the jars from the canner, and let it cool.

10) Serve!

Nutrition:

- Calories: 88

- Protein: 0 g

- Fiber: 0 g

- Fat: 0 g

- Carbs: 23 g

53. Orange Pineapple Marmalade

Preparation Time: 35 Minutes

Cooking Time: 1 Hour 20 Minutes

Servings: 4 pint jars

Ingredients:

- 2 Cans (8 ounces each) drained crushed pineapple

- 2 Medium oranges

- 2 Tablespoons lemon juice

- 4 Cups sugar

Directions:

1) Wash four one-cup plastic containers and lids, and sterilize them with boiling water. Dry and set aside.

2) Scrape the orange peel, and set aside. Peel off the orange, discarding the white membrane, section the flesh and remove the seeds.

3) Combine in a food processor, the orange sections and zest. Cover and pulse until the orange turns into small bits.

4) Place lemon juice, the orange mixture, sugar and pineapple in a 2 1/2 quart microwave safe bowl with a wide bottom.

5) Microwave the mixture without a cover on high for 2 to 2 1/2 minutes.

6) Stir and heat until bubbly, stir again and microwave for another 1 1/2 to 2 minutes until the middle part is bubbly. Stir and heat for two more minutes, stir often and let cool for ten minutes.

7) Ladle the hot marmalade into plastic containers, leaving a 1/2 inch allowance from the tops.

8) Wipe off the edges with paper towels. Let it cool for 1 hour. Cover

9) the plastic containers and let it stand for four hours at room temperature.

10) Keep refrigerated or keep frozen for up to one year.

11) Thaw for an hour or so in the refrigerator before you serve the marmalade.

12) Enjoy!

Nutrition:

- Calories: 104

- Protein: 0 g

- Fiber: 0 g

- Fat: 1 g

- Carbs: 27 g

54. Cherry Marmalade

Preparation time: 20 minutes

Cooking time: 30 minutes

Serves: 4 pints

Ingredients:

- 4 tbsps. lime

- 4 cup cherries

- 2/3 cup peeled and chopped orange

- 3-1/2 cup sugar

Directions:

1) Take a large pan and mix cherries, orange and juice in it. Make them boil at medium heat. Low the flame and add cove with gentle boiling with frequent stirring for 20 minutes. Keep boiling with

2) slow stirring.

3) Now boil hard with frequent stirring as the mixture gets gel like, for about 30 minutes. Remove the flame.

4) Pour the hot marmalade into sterilized jars. Remove the air bubble by adding more marmalade. Seal them with lids.

Nutrition:

- Calories 56

- Fat: 0 g

- Carbs: 13 g

- Protein 1 g

Chutneys

55. Rhubarb Chutney

Preparation Time: 15 minutes

Cooking Time: 15 minutes

Servings: 6 pint jars

Ingredients:

- 8 cups sliced rhubarb

- 6 cups sliced onion

- 2 cups raisins

- 7 cups light brown sugar

- 4 cups apple cider vinegar

- 2 tbsps. salt

- 2 tsps. cinnamon

- 2 tsps. ginger

- 1 tsp. ground cloves

- 1/8 tsp. cayenne pepper

Directions:

1) Mix all the components together in a large pot.

2) Boil, then simmer gently until the liquid is slightly thickened.

3) Pour into sterile jars and wipe the rims.

4) Tighten the lids and process in a hot water bath for 10 minutes.

Nutrition:

- Calories: 58

- Fat: 1g

- Carbs: 12g Protein 0g

56. Mango Chutney

Preparation Time: 15 minutes

Cooking Time: 45 minutes

Servings: 4 pint jars

Ingredients:

- 6 cups sliced green mangos

- 1/2 lb. fresh ginger

- 31/2 cups currants

- 8 cups sugar

- 2cups vinegar

- 3 cups ground cayenne pepper

- 1 cup salt

Directions:

1) Peel the ginger and halve it.

2) Slice one half of the ginger into thin slices; chop the other half of the ginger roughly.

3) Grind the sliced ginger with half of the currants using a blender until well combined. Place all in a saucepan, except the mangoes.

4) Cook over medium heat for 15 minutes.

5) Meanwhile, to set 6 cups, cut, halve, pit, and slice the green mangos.

6) After 15 minutes of cooking, attach the mangos and parboil for another 30 minutes until the mangos are tender.

7) Pour into shot glasses, clean the rims, and screw the lids and rings together.

8) Use the boiling water bath process: pints and quarts for 10 minutes in both.

Nutrition:

- Calories 37

- Fat: 0g

- Carbs: 12g

- Protein 0g

57. Rhubarb Cherry Chutney

Preparation Time: 15 minutes

Cooking Time: 35 minutes

Servings: 6 pint jars

Ingredients:

- 2 lbs. chopped fresh rhubarb

- 2 cups chopped cherries

- 1 chopped apple

- 1 chopped red onion

- 1 chopped celery rib

- 2 minced garlic cloves

- 1tbsp. chopped crystallized ginger

- 2 cups brown sugar

- 1 cup red wine vinegar

- 3/4 tsp. ground cinnamon

- 1/2 tsp. ground coriander

- 1/4 tsp. ground cloves

Directions:

1) In a 6-quart stockpot, combine all ingredients and allow to boil.

2) Simmer 30 minute while uncovered.

3) Transfer to covered containers. If freezing, use freezer-safe containers and fill to within 1/2-inch of tops.

4) Freeze up to 12 months or refrigerate up to 3 weeks. Before serving, thaw frozen salsa in the refrigerator.

Nutrition:

- Calories: 102

- Carbs: 27g

- Fat: 0g

- Protein: 0g

58. Raisin Pear Chutney

Preparation Time: 15 minutes

Cooking Time: 20 minutes

Servings: 2 pint jars

Ingredients:

- 2 cups cider vinegar

- 11/4 cups packed brown sugar

- 3 lbs. unpeeled ripe pears, diced

- 1 chopped onion

- 1cup raisins

- 21 tsps. ground cinnamon

- 1 tsp. ground cloves

- 1 minced garlic clove

- 1 tsp. cayenne pepper

Directions:

1) In a saucepan, bring brown sugar and vinegar to a boil.

2) Stir in the remaining ingredients and return to a boil.

3) Reduce heat and let simmer uncovered for 2 hours to 2 hours 15 minutes until chutney reaches desired consistency.

4) Carefully scoop hot mixture into hot sterilized pint jars, leaving 1/4-inch headspace. Remove air bubbles and, if necessary, adjust headspace by adding more hot mixture. Wipe the rims carefully. Place tops on jars and screw on bands until fingertip tight.

5) Place jars into canner with boiling water, ensuring that they are completely covered with water. Let boil for 15 minutes. Remove jars and cool.

Nutrition:

- Calories: 152

- Carbs: 40g

- Fat: 0g

- Protein: 1g

59. Cucumber Relish with Pepper

Preparation Time: 14 minutes

Cooking Time: 13 minutes

Servings: 4 pint jars

Ingredients:

- 4 pounds (1.8 kg) finely chopped pickling cucumbers

- 1/2 cup canning salt

- 1/2 cup white vinegar

- 21/3 cups sugar

- 4 tablespoons mustard seeds

- 3 cloves garlic, finely minced

- 2 tablespoons celery seeds

- 2 cups diced red bell pepper

- 2 cups finely chopped white onion

Directions:

1) Place cucumbers in a large glass bowl and stir in the salt. Allow them to sit on the counter at room temperature for 4 hours.

2) Drain cucumbers and rinse in a colander under cold water, squeezing out the excess water with your hands.

3) Combine garlic, sugar, mustard seeds, celery seeds, and white vinegar in a saucepan and bring to a boil.

4) Reduce heat and stir in cucumbers, onions, and peppers, then return to a full boil.

5) Reduce heat and simmer the mixture for 10 minutes.

6) Ladle the hot relish into pint or half-pint jars, allowing 1/2 inch of headspace.

7) Secure the jars and process in a hot water bath canner for 10 minutes, adjusting for altitude.

Nutrition:

- Calories: 88

- Protein: 0 g

- Fiber: 0 g

- Fat: 0 g

- Carbs: 23 g

60. Mango Chutney with Raisin

Preparation Time: 19 minutes

Cooking Time: 30 minutes

Servings: 6 pint jars

Ingredients:

- 11 cups or 4 pounds (1.8 kg) chopped unripe (hard) mango, either

- Tommy Atkins or Kent varieties

- 21/2 cups or 3/4 pounds finely chopped yellow onion

- 21/2 tablespoons grated fresh ginger

- 11/2 tablespoons finely chopped fresh garlic

- 41/2 cups sugar

- 3 cups white distilled vinegar (5%)

- 21/2 cups golden raisins

- 11 teaspoon canning salt

- 4 teaspoons chili powder

Directions:

1) 1. Wash all produce well. Peel, core and chop mangoes into 3/4-inch cubes.

2) Slice mango cubes in food processor, using 6 one-second pulses per food processor batch.

3) By hand, skin and dice onion, finely chop garlic, and grate ginger.

4) Merge sugar and vinegar in an 8- to 10-quart stockpot.

5) Set to a boil, and boil 5 minutes.

6) Attach all other ingredients and set back to a boil.

7) Set heat and parboil 25 minutes, stirring occasionally.

8) Fill hot chutney into hot pint or half-pint jars, leaving 1/2-inch headspace.

9) Detach air bubbles and adjust headspace if needed.

10) Clean the jars with a dampened clean paper towel.

11) Adjust lids and process.

Nutrition:

- Calories: 47

- Fat: 0g

- Carbs: 11.1g Protein 0g

61. Garlicky Lime Chutney

Preparation Time: 10 minutes

Cooking Time: 60 minutes

Servings: 3 pint jars

Ingredients:

- 12 limes, scrubbed and cut into 1/2-inch dice

- 12 garlic cloves, thinly sliced lengthwise

- 1 (4-inch) piece fresh ginger, peeled and thinly sliced

- 8 green chili peppers (jalapeños or Serrano's), stemmed, seeded, and thinly sliced 1 tablespoon chili powder

- 1 cup distilled white vinegar

- 3/4 cup sugar

Directions:

1) Prepare a hot water bath. Bring the jars in it to keep warm. Clean the lids and rings in hot, soapy water, and set aside.

2) In a medium saucepan, combine the limes, garlic, ginger, chiles, and chili powder, stir well, and bring to a simmer.

3) Add the vinegar and sugar, return to a simmer, and cook, stirring occasionally, until the limes are tender and the mixture is thick to mound when dropped from a spoon, about 70 minutes. Remove from the heat.

4) Ladle the chutney into the prepared jars, leaving 1/4 inch of headspace. Use a nonmetallic utensil to free any air bubbles. Clean the rims and seal with the lids and rings.

5) Set the jars in a hot water bath for 20 minutes. Set off the heat and let the jars rest in the water bath.

6) Carefully detach the jars from the hot water canner. Set aside to cool for 12 hours.

7) Check the lids for proper seals. Remove the rings, wipe the jars, label and date them, and transfer to a cupboard or pantry.

8) For the best flavor, allow the chutney to rest for 3 days before serving. Set in refrigerator any jars that don't seal properly, and use within 6 weeks. Properly secure jars will last in the

cupboard for 12 months. Once opened, refrigerate and consume within 6 weeks.

Nutrition:

- Calories: 58

- Fat: 1g

- Carbs: 12g

- Protein 0g

62. Pungent Tomato Pear Chutney

Preparation Time: 45 minutes

Cooking Time: 10 minutes

Servings: 5 pint jars

Ingredients:

- 2 lbs. pears, peeled, chopped

- 2lbs. tomatoes, peeled, seeded, chopped

- 1cup finely chopped seeded jalapeno peppers

- 2 cups chopped onions

- 4 tsp. minced fresh ginger root

- 1-2 tsp. crushed red pepper flakes

- 1 tsp. ground mustard

- 1 cup cider vinegar

- 1 cup brown sugar

Directions:

1) In a Dutch oven, combine all ingredients. Bring to a boil.

2) Reduce heat and simmer for 45-60 minutes, uncovered, until thickened, stirring occasionally.

3) Carefully scoop hot mixture into hot sterilized half-pint jars, leaving 1/2-inch headspace. Remove air bubbles and if necessary, adjust headspace by adding hot mixture. Wipe the rims carefully. Place tops on jars and screw on bands until fingertip tight.

4) Place jars into canner with boiling water, ensuring that they are completely covered with water. Let boil for 10 minutes. Remove jars and cool.

Nutrition:

- Carbohydrates: 22 g

- Fat: 0 g

- Protein: 1 g

- Sodium: 8 mg

- Calories: 88

63. Cilantro Chutney Recipe

Preparation Time: 45 minutes

Cooking Time: 10 minutes

Servings: 5 pint jars

Ingredients:

- 1/2 cup of yogurt (this can be omitted or replaced with a veganbased version of yogurt)

- Lemon juice, three tablespoons

- Cilantro with stems removed (small branches can be left intact), one bunch

- Mint leaves, about one cup packed

- Ginger, sliced (2 teaspoons)

- Sea salt, 1/2 teaspoon

- One garlic clove

- One medium-sized jalapeno, sliced finely

- Sugar, 1/2 teaspoon

Directions:

1) Merge all the ingredients above in a blender with one tablespoon of water.

2) Taste and add more spice as needed, then pour it into a sterilized jar and store in the refrigerator. If you want to substitute the yogurt for a non-dairy alternative, you can add coconut or soy-based yogurt. Tofu is another option to consider.

3) If you wish to preserve for a longer time frame, omit the yogurt entirely and store the chutney in a jar for up to one month in your refrigerator.

Nutrition:

- Calories: 88

- Carbs: 22g

- Fat: 0g

- Protein: 1g

64. Indian Apple Chutney

Preparation Time: 14 minutes

Cooking Time: 20 minutes

Servings: 6 pint jars

Ingredients:

- 2 pounds of apples (medium in size)

- 1 cup of diced onions (finely diced)

- Allspice, two teaspoons

- Ginger, ground or fresh, about two tablespoons Raisins, about 7 cups or two pounds

- Red bell pepper, chopped finely, about one cup

- Mustard seeds, about three tablespoons

- Curry powder, about two teaspoons

- Pickling salt, two teaspoons

- 1 clove of garlic, crushed

- 2 hot peppers, seeds removed and diced finely

- 4 cups of malt vinegar

- Brown sugar, about 4 cups (or less, if you prefer less sugar)

Directions:

1) To prepare, wash, and scrub the apples, then peel, core, and slice. Place the apples in a large cooking pot and cover with water. Wash and slice the onions, removing all the skin, and add to the cooking pot.

2) Repeat the same process with the peppers and add them into the pot with the onions and apples. Pour the remaining ingredients into the cooking pot, including the malt vinegar, and bring the contents to a boil. Once this point is reached,

cook for about 2 minutes, then reduce to a simmer and stir often.

3) Continue this process until the apples are tender, which can take up to one hour. Place the mixture into sterilized jars and adjust to allow for one inch of space at the top. Clean down the rims of the jars before scooping the contents of the chutney into the jars.

4) Place the lids on tightly and process in a water bath canner for 1011 minutes. Allow the jars to cool on a wire rack or cloth overnight, then store in a pantry or fruit cellar for up to one month.

Nutrition:

- Calories: 47

- Fat: 0g

- Carbs: 11.1g

- Protein 0g

65. Plum Tomato Chutney

Preparation Time: 15 minutes

Cooking Time: 15 minutes

Servings: 4 pint jars

Ingredients:

- 4 tomatoes, chopped

- plums, seeded and chopped

- 2green chilies, chopped

- 4tablespoons fresh ginger, grated

- 1teaspoon lemon zest

- Juice of 1 lemon

- 2 bay leaves

- Pinch of salt

- 1/2 cup plus 2 tbsp. brown sugar

- 2 teaspoons vinegar

- Pinch black pepper

- 4 tsps. vegetable oil

Directions:

1) Heat the oil in a deep saucepan. Add the bay leaves, ginger and green chilies, and stir. Add the tomatoes, plums. Add the salt, zest, lemon juice and vinegar. Stir in the sugar and pepper, cover, and cook for 3 minutes.

2) Spoon the chutney into sterilized jars, leaving a 1/2 inch headspace. Wipe the edge of the jar rim clean and add the lid.

3) Process these in a boiling water bath for 10 minutes.

Nutrition:

- Calories 70

- Fat: 0 g

- Carbs: 31 g

- Protein 1 g

66. Curried Apple Chutney

Preparation Time: 15 minutes

Cooking Time: 15 minutes

Servings: 10 pint jars

Ingredients:

- 2 quarts apples, peeled, cored and chopped

- 2 pounds raisins

- 4 cups brown sugar

- 1 cup onion, chopped

- 1 cup sweet pepper, chopped

- 3 tbsps. mustard seed

- 2 tbsps. ground ginger

- 2 tsps. allspice

- 2 tsps. curry powder

- 2 tsps. salt

- 2 hot red peppers, chopped

- 1 clove garlic, minced

- 4 cups vinegar

Directions:

1) In a large saucepan, mix all of the ingredients together. Set to a boil and simmer for 1 hour.

2) Spoon the chutney into sterilized jars, leaving a 1/2 inch headspace. Wipe the jars' edge rim clean and add the lid. Set jars in a water bath for 10 minutes.

Nutrition:

- Calories 23

- Fat: 0 g

- Carbs: 11 g Protein 0 g

67. Fruit Chutney

Preparation Time: 15 minutes

Cooking Time: 15 minutes

Servings: 3 pint jars

Ingredients:

- 1 tbsp. canola oil

- 4 cups onion, chopped

- 1 tbsp. garlic, minced

- 8 cups prepared fresh fruits, peeled including pears, peaches, tomatoes and apples

- 1 cup mixed dried fruits, chopped

- 1 cup granulated sugar

- 1 cup white vinegar

- 1 cup water

- 1 tsp. crushed red pepper

- 1 tsp. salt

Directions:

1) In a large pan, warmth the oil and cook the onion about 6 minutes. Attach the garlic and stir for 30 seconds. Stir in the fresh fruit, dried fruit, sugar, vinegar, water, red pepper flakes, and salt. Set this to a boil, stirring often, then reduce heat and simmer for 30 minutes.

2) Spoon the chutney into sterilized jars to within 1/2 inch of the rim. Clean the rims and set the lids on each jar. Process the jars in a water bath for 15 minutes.

Nutrition:

- Calories 47

- Fat: 0 g

- Carbs: 11.1 g

- Protein 0 g

68. Green Tomato Chutney

Preparation Time: 15 minutes

Cooking Time: 15 minutes

Servings: 3 pint jars

Ingredients:

- 2-1/2 pounds firm green tomatoes, chopped

- 1-1/4 cups brown sugar, packed

- 1 cup red onion, chopped

- 1cup golden raisins

- 1cup cider vinegar

- 2 tbsps. candied ginger, minced

- 1 tbsp. mustard seeds

- 1 tsp. chili pepper flakes

- 1 tsp. fennel seeds

- 1 tsp. salt

- 1/2 tsp. ground allspice

- 1/8 tsp. ground cloves

- 1 cinnamon stick

- Pinch of ground nutmeg

Directions:

1) Set all of the ingredients in a 4-quart pot. Bring to a boil and then reduce to a simmer. Secure the pot and cook for 45 minutes.

2) Spoon the chutney into sterilized jars, filling them to 1/4 inch from the rim. Wipe the rims clean and set lids on the jars. Process for 15 minutes in a boiling water bath.

Nutrition:

- Calories 18.2

- Fat: 0 g

- Carbs: 6 g

- Protein 0 g

69. Cantaloupe Chutney

Preparation Time: 15 minutes

Cooking Time: 90 minutes

Servings: 3 pint jars

Ingredients:

- 2 Medium cantaloupes

- 1 pound of dried apricots

- 1 fresh hot chili

- 2 cups of raisins

- 1 tsp. ground cloves

- 1 tsp. ground nutmeg

- 2 tbsps. salt

- 2 tbsps. mustard seed

- 1/4 cup fresh ginger, chopped

- 3 cloves garlic

- 4-1/2 cups apple cider vinegar

- 2-1/4 cups brown sugar

- 4 onions

- 1/2 cup orange juice

- 2 tbsps. orange zest

Directions:

1) Thinly cut the apricots and put them into a large bowl.

2) Slice the ginger and garlic thinly, and add to the dish.

3) Stir in chili, seed, and dice, and attach to the pot.

4) Attach raisins, cloves, cinnamon, nutmeg, and mustard seeds.

5) Mix together and set aside.

6) Merge the vinegar and sugar in a non-reactive pot or kettle; bring to boil over medium heat.

7) Attach mixture to the pot in a bowl and return to a moderate simmer.

8) Keep simmer for 45 minutes. Do not deck the pot.

9) Meanwhile, onions are sliced and placed in a bowl.

10) Cantaloupes fifth, peel, and seed.

11) Set the fruit into cubes of 1/2 Add onions.

12) In cup, attach orange juice and zest; mix well.

13) Once the vinegar mixture has ended 45 minutes of cooking time, add the cantaloupe mixture to the bowl, bring it back to a cooler, and start cooking for another 45 minutes or until thickened at the simmer.

14) Pour into hot glasses, clean the rims, screw the lids and rings together.

15) Boiling water bath process: pints and quarts 10 minutes in both.

Nutrition:

- Calories 54

- Fat: 0 g

- Carbs: 14 g

- Protein 1 g

70. Spicy Green Tomato Chutney

Preparation Time: 15 minutes

Cooking Time: 15 minutes

Servings: 3 pint jars

Ingredients:

- 2-1/2 cups spiced cider vinegar

- 3 cups shallots, finely chopped

- 2 quarters small green tomatoes, peeled and thinly sliced

- 1 tsp. celery salt

- 4 cups finely chopped apples

- 2 sweet red or green peppers

- Dry, hot chilies (four to six depending on heat strength)

- 2-1/4 cups brown sugar

- 2 cups ripe tomatoes, peeled and chopped salt

Directions

1) Combine 2-1/2 cups of apple cider vinegar, 1 stick of cinnamon, 1 teaspoon of allspice, whole cloves, black peppercorns, and frac12; teaspoon ground nutmeg in a medium ability boiling pot.

2) Set the fire on, and nearly get it to the boil.

3) Detach from the heat immediately and allow to cool down to room temperature.

4) Strain before applying to the chutney.

5) Black tomatoes to be peeled:

6) Place bowl, pot, or kettle in heat-proof.

7) Pour over boiling water to cover, letting them rest for three minutes.

8) Pierce peel with a sharp knife's tip and pull off the skin.

9) Slice very thinly on those tomatoes.

10) Pour in a colander over a tub, or green tomato slices with salt in a sink plate.

11) Let them drain for two hours.

In the meantime:

1) Skin, chop the apples sweet, core, and finely to make 4 cups.

2) A place to ready for use in acidulated water.

3) Clean shallots, then finely chop them to make 3 cups.

4) Prepare sweet peppers by washing, seeding, halving, and de rib.

5) Place under broiler or over open flames until the skin is charred and fleece away. Remove peppers; slice them thinly.

6) Place the chilies in a bag with cheesecloth.

7) Rinse green tomatoes at the end of two hours.

8) Combine green tomato slices, spiced strained vinegar, shallots, apples, hot chili bag, brown sugar, and celery salt in a large bowl.

9) Set to a boil, cook for 15 minutes or until most of the liquid has evaporated.

10) Remove broiled, ripe tomatoes, and sweet peppers.

11) Simmer for about an hour, until dark.

12) Remove the bag of chili.

13) Pour into shot glasses, clean the rims, screw the lids and rings together.

14) Boiling water bath process: pints and quarts 10 minutes in both.

Nutrition:

- Calories 236

- Fat: 0 g

- Carbs: 22 g;

- Protein 0.6 g

71. Black Currant

Preparation Time: 15 minutes

Cooking Time: 30 minutes

Servings: 3 pint jars

Ingredients:

- 41/2 cups black currants, crushed

- 1/4 cup lemon juice

- 3 cups granulated sugar

- 1 cup water

- 1 tablespoon lemon zest

- Pinch of salt

Directions

1) Combine the ingredients in a deep saucepan or cooking pot.

2) Boil the mixture and cook for about 30 minutes over medium heat until firm and thick. Stir continually to prevent scorching.

3) Spill the hot mixture into pre-sterilized jars directly or with a jar funnel. Keep headspace of 1/4 inch from the jar top.

4) To detach tiny air bubbles, insert a nonmetallic spatula and stir the mixture gently.

5) Clean the sealing edges with a cloth. Secure the jars with the lids and adjust the bands/rings to seal and prevent any leakage.

6) Set the jars in a hot water bath for 10 minutes.

7) Set the jars in a cool, dry and dark place. Allow them to cool down completely.

8) Store in your refrigerator.

Nutrition:

- Calories 47

- Fat: 0 g

- Carbs: 11.1 g

- Protein 0 g

72. Watermelon Lemon

Preparation Time: 15 minutes

Cooking Time: 30 minutes

Servings: 3 pint jars

Ingredients:

- 2 pounds watermelon, peeled, seeded and cubed

- 3 cups white sugar

- 3 lemons, unpeeled, sliced and seeded

Directions:

1) In a deep saucepan or cooking pot, merge the watermelon cubes, lemons and sugar.

2) Boil the mixture; cook for about 2 hours over medium heat until firm and thick. Stir continually to prevent scorching.

3) Spill the hot mixture into pre-sterilized jars directly or with a jar funnel. Keep headspace of 1/4 inch from the jar top.

4) To detach tiny air bubbles, insert a nonmetallic spatula and stir the mixture gently.

5) Clean the sealing edges with a damp cloth. Secure the jars with the lids and adjust the bands/rings to seal and prevent any leakage.

6) Set the jars in a hot water bath for 10 minutes.

7) Set the jars in a cool, dry and dark place. Allow them to cool down completely.

8) Store in your refrigerator.

Nutrition:

- Calories: 36.1

- Total fat: 0g

- Carbs: 10g

- Protein: 0g

- Sugars: 9g

- Fiber: 0g

73. Tangy Tomato

Preparation Time: 15 minutes

Cooking Time: 30 minutes

Servings: 3-4 pint jars

Ingredients:

- 1 cup sugar

- 3/4 cup honey

- 2 medium lemons, unpeeled, chopped and seeded

- 21/2 pounds yellow tomatoes

- 2 ounces ginger, grated

Directions:

1) In a deep saucepan or cooking pot, merge the water and tomatoes.

2) Boil the mixture; simmer over low heat to soften the tomatoes.

3) Peel the skin, remove the seeds, and finely chop the tomatoes.

4) In a deep saucepan or cooking pot, merge the chopped tomatoes, honey and sugar.

5) Set aside for a few hours.

6) Add the lemons and ginger.

7) Boil the mixture; cook over medium heat until firm and thick. Swirl continually to prevent scorching.

8) Spill the hot mixture into pre-sterilized jars directly or with a jar funnel. Keep headspace of 1/4 inch from the jar top.

9) To free tiny air bubbles, set a nonmetallic spatula and swirl the mixture.

10) Clean the sealing edges with a damp cloth. Secure the jars with the lids and adjust the bands/rings to seal and prevent any leakage.

11) Set the jars in a hot water bath for 5 minutes.

12) Bring the jars in a cool, dry and dark place. Allow them to cool down completely.

13) Store in your refrigerator.

Nutrition:

- Calories: 36.1

- Total fat: 0g

- Carbs: 10g

- Protein: 0g

- Sugars: 9g

- Fiber: 0g

- Sodium: 227.1mg

- Potassium: 0mg

74. Delicious Strawberry Preserve

Preparation Time: 15 minutes

Cooking Time: 15 minutes

Servings: 3-4 pint jars

Ingredients:

- 3 cups granulated sugar

- 4 cups strawberries, halved

- 1 tablespoon + 1 teaspoon lemon juice

Directions:

1) In a deep saucepan or cooking pot, merge the sugar and strawberries.

2) Set aside for a few hours.

3) Warmth the mixture and mix in the lemon juice.

4) Boil the mixture; cook for about 7–8 minutes over medium heat until firm and thick. Swirl continually.

5) Spill the hot mixture into pre-sterilized jars directly or with a jar funnel. Keep headspace of 1/4 inch from the jar top.

6) To detach tiny air bubbles, insert a nonmetallic spatula and stir the mixture gently.

7) Clean the sealing edges with a damp cloth. Secure the jars with the lids and adjust the bands/rings to seal and prevent any leakage.

8) Set the jars in a cool, dry and dark place. Allow them to cool down completely.

9) Store in your refrigerator.

Nutrition:

- Calories: 49

- Fat: 0.2g

- Carbs: 8.7g,

- Protein: 3.6g

- Sugars: 4.9g